PAINT YOUR
FUTURE

66 Inspirational Poems and Devotions:
Read Them, Share Them, and
Let Them Transform Your Life.

EDITH PERRY

WestBow
PRESS®
A DIVISION OF THOMAS NELSON
& ZONDERVAN

WestBow Press books may be ordered through booksellers or by contacting:

WestBow Press
A Division of Thomas Nelson & Zondervan
1663 Liberty Drive
Bloomington, IN 47403
www.westbowpress.com
844-714-3454

All Scripture quotations are taken from the King James Version.

ISBN: 978-1-6642-5014-7 (sc)
ISBN: 978-1-6642-5013-0 (e)

Library of Congress Control Number: 2021923394

Print information available on the last page.

WestBow Press rev. date: 1/10/2022

CONTENTS

POEMS FOR RIGHTEOUS LIVING

Are You Ready?

Are you ready to accept your responsibility in Jesus Christ?

Ready to accept Jesus as your Lord and Savior?

Ready to obey the laws of God?

Are you ready to reap the promises God gave to His people?

Ready to transform your mind and become Christ-like?

Ready to live a life that offers peace, joy,
and happiness in the Holy Spirit?

Are you ready to be born again?

Ready to use your spiritual gifts?

People of God, when will you be ready to
serve God with all, our heart, mind, and soul?

It is time for you to stop getting ready and
be ready when, Jesus comes back for his church.

Paint Your Future
with
Practical Points for Reflection

List three words that best describe what this poem means to your life.

1. _____.

2. _____.

3. _____.

After reading this poem, list three characteristics you want to change for the better.

1. _____.

2. _____.

3. _____.

Take- Action

Do things that will shape your future.

1. Do not put off today for tomorrow.
2. Listen to wise men and women.
3. Make your life goals a priority.
4. Set a date to complete a task.
5. Have a mind to grow and stop settling for less.
6. Start small, then increase.

Revelation 22:12-13
And behold, I come quickly, and my reward is with me,
to give every man according as his work shall be.

I am an Eagle

When your associates and friends disassociate themselves
from you, tell yourselves you are an eagle.

When you are being mistreated and talked about,
tell yourself that you are an eagle.

When you desire to correct the wrongs in your life
with the help of God's word, tell yourself you are an eagle.

When people are jealous of your life with Jesus,
tell yourself, you are an eagle.

No matter what trials or tribulation come against you,
tell yourself, you are an eagle.

When you return to the old you to get to the new you,
in Jesus Christ, tell yourself you are an eagle.

When you are no longer embracing the things

of this world, tell yourself you are an eagle.

When you see yourself soaring alone, you are an eagle.

When the fruits of the spirit shine bright in your
spiritual walk with Jesus, you are an eagle.

When God gives you his Holy Spirit and spiritual gifts,
you are not just an eagle, you are a Holy Eagle.

Paint Your Future
with
Practical Points for Reflection

List three words that best describe what this poem means to your life.

1. _____.

2. _____.

3. _____.

After reading this poem, list three characteristics you want to change for the better.

1. _____.

2. _____.

3. _____.

Take- Action
Do things that will shape your future.

1. Do not put off today for tomorrow.
2. Listen to wise men and women.
3. Make your life goals a priority.
4. Set a date to complete a task.
5. Have a mind to grow and stop settling for less.
6. Start small, then increase.

Isaiah 40:31
But they that wait upon the LORD shall renew their strength;
they shall mount up with wings as eagles; they shall run,
and not be weary, and they shall walk, and not faint.

Choose

One day you became tired of sin.

You decided to choose Jesus to win.

You did not know Jesus was real until you chose him to

help you from drinking gin.

What a relief to be released from the world's bondage soup

of just for us sins.

What a mighty God we serve full of truth and kindness.

With Jesus's help, you no longer need to guess about sin.

Thank you, Jesus, for your servant pastors and teachers for

teaching us how to defeat the devil and win.

Choose Jesus because he will give you his

best unlike the world who will lie to you just to

give you less.

Paint Your Future
with
Practical Points for Reflection

List three words that best describe what this poem means to your life.

1. _____.

2. _____.

3. _____.

After reading this poem, list three characteristics you want to change for the better.

1. _____.

2. _____.

3. _____.

Take- Action
Do things that will shape your future.

1. Do not put off today for tomorrow.
2. Listen to wise men and women.
3. Make your life goals a priority.
4. Set a date to complete a task.
5. Have a mind to grow and stop settling for less.
6. Start small, then increase.

Proverbs 14:12
There is a way which seems right unto a man,
but the end thereof are the ways of death.

Claim and Erase

Lord, I claim victory and erase defeat.

I claim love and erase hate.

I claim understanding and erase ignorance.

I claim wealth and erase poverty.

Lord, I claim health and erase sickness.

I claim work and erase laziness.

I claim a relationship in Christ and erase loneliness.

I claim a spirited-filled life and erase a corruptible life.

Lord, I claim healing and erase suffering.

I claim spiritual gifts and erase selfish gifts.

I claim eternal life and erase a sinner's life.

I claim humility and erase pride of life.

Lord, I claim forgiveness and erase animosity.

I claim the truth and erase false doctrine.

I claim freedom and erase addiction.

Children of God, let us claim everything of

God and erase everything evil.

Paint Your Future
with
Practical Points for Reflection

List three words that best describe what this poem means to your life.

1. _____.

2. _____.

3. _____.

After reading this poem, list three characteristics you want to change for the better.

1. _____.

2. _____.

3. _____.

Take-Action
Do things that will shape your future.

1. Do not put off today for tomorrow.
2. Listen to wise men and women.
3. Make your life goals a priority.
4. Set a date to complete a task.
5. Have a mind to grow and stop settling for less.
6. Start small, then increase.

James 1:5
"If any of you lack wisdom, let him ask of God, that giveth to all men liberally,
and upbraid not, and it shall be given him."

Closer to God

Temptations are all around us, yet we are getting closer to God.

Sometimes, your thoughts are things of this world, but your
spiritual thoughts put you closer to God.

You continuously pray for God to take away things in your
life that will keep you from getting closer to God.

We know it will be the teaching of the Holy Spirit
that will allow us to, get closer to God.

Oh, what a joyful and sometimes sorrowful life
we live just to get closer to God.

We know why our light shines on us in and out of the church,

it is because we are getting closer to God.

Anytime you get closer to God, the devil will put an obstacle in your way.

It is the promises of God that draw us closer to Him.

Getting closer to God allows us to trust the Holy Spirit through

our faith to help change things in our lives.

Getting closer to God helps children of God believe
in the working, miracles of God.

Getting closer to God helps win souls for his kingdom.

Getting closer to Jesus helps you to believe in God.

Getting closer to God settles it.

Paint Your Future
with
Practical Points for Reflection

List three words that best describe what this poem means to your life.

1. _____.

2. _____.

3. _____.

After reading this poem, list three characteristics you want to change for the better.

1. _____.

2. _____.

3. _____.

Take- Action

Do things that will shape your future.

1. Do not put off today for tomorrow.
2. Listen to wise men and women.
3. Make your life goals a priority.
4. Set a date to complete a task.
5. Have a mind to grow and stop settling for less.
6. Start small, then increase.

Psalms 73:28
"But it is good for me to draw near to God:
I have put my trust in the Lord GOD,
that I may declare all thy works."

Comfort Zone

What shall we do now that we are no longer in our comfort zone?

We may feel lost without our comfort zone.

What shall we do when we realize
our comfort zone is no longer with us?

Maybe it is the time, place, and people who have
taken us away from our comfort zone.

We should pray and ask God to take us back to our comfort zone.

We should not rely on our comfort zone to the point we forget to

have faith in the power and might of Jesus Christ.

Our comfort zone should be in the love and
peace of Jesus Christ and not in the things of this world.

Comfort zone, comfort zone, comfort zone where art thou?

It is in our heart, mind, and soul for those
who believe Jesus is the Messiah.

Paint Your Future
with
Practical Points for Reflection

List three words that best describe what this poem means to your life.

1. _____.

2. _____.

3. _____.

After reading this poem, list three characteristics you want to change for the better.

1. _____.

2. _____.

3. _____.

Take- Action
Do things that will shape your future.

1. Do not put off today for tomorrow.
2. Listen to wise men and women.
3. Make your life goals a priority.
4. Set a date to complete a task.
5. Have a mind to grow and stop settling for less.
6. Start small, then increase.

Matthew 11:28
"Come unto me, all ye that labor
and are heavily laden, and I will give you rest."

God Fearing Choices

Children of God need to come up higher,

in Christ by making Godfearing choices.

Choose spiritual gifts that last a lifetime.

Choose a lifetime of blessings.

Choose to walk in the spirit of God and not,

in your fleshy desires.

God-fearing choices will give you a life of victory over sin.

Choose joy and peace for your life.

God-fearing choices will bring you closer to God.

God-fearing choices will allow you to live a righteous life.

God-fearing choices will bring about repentance.

God-fearing choices will allow you to love others.

God-fearing choices will bond the devil.

People of God either chose God-fearing choices,

and live or make foolish choices and die.

Which are you?

Paint Your Future
with
Practical Points for Reflection

List three words that best describe what this poem means to your life.

1. _____.

2. _____.

3. _____.

After reading this poem, list three characteristics you want to change for the better.

1. _____.

2. _____.

3. _____.

Take- Action
Do things that will shape your future.

1. Do not put off today for tomorrow.
2. Listen to wise men and women.
3. Make your life goals a priority.
4. Set a date to complete a task.
5. Have a mind to grow and stop settling for less.
6. Start small, then increase.

Proverbs 19:21
"There are many devices in a man's heart;
nevertheless the counsel of the LORD, that shall stand."

Growing Up

We come to God drinking milk,
and a year later, we are, on puree food.

Three years later, we can digest ground food
that allow, us to hear God's word by faith.

The spiritual gifts of knowledge and understanding,

allow saints to eat chop food.

The chop food stage tells us God's word is

being implanted into our hearts

Our spiritual growth is ready for whole food,

when we are submissive,

to God's laws and principles.

The word of God is food for our souls.

Growing up in Jesus Christ is rewarding

and forever nurturing,

our mind, body, and soul.

Growing up, Hallelujah

Paint Your Future
with
Practical Points for Reflection

List three words that best describe what this poem means to your life.

1. _____.

2. _____.

3. _____.

After reading this poem, list three characteristics you want to change for the better.

1. _____.

2. _____.

3. _____.

Take- Action
Do things that will shape your future.

1. Do not put off today for tomorrow.
2. Listen to wise men and women.
3. Make your life goals a priority.
4. Set a date to complete a task.
5. Have a mind to grow and stop settling for less.
6. Start small, then increase.

1 Corinthians 14:20
"Brethren, be not children in understanding:
howbeit in malice be ye children, but in understanding be men."

It's Better

It is better to walk in the light of God than to walk with a rich thief.

It is better to repent from sin than to rejoice in vainglory.

It is better to be under the laws of God than to plot and do evil.

It is better to fear God than to trust in the pride of men.

It is better to live for the sake of righteousness than to be deceitful by fools.

It is better to put on humility, love, and peace than to be clothed with hate.

It is better to have a controlled tongue than a lying tongue.

It is better to be spiritual-minded than evil-minded.

It is better to be found in the presence of the Lord than to be found corruptible.

It is better to be accepted by God's grace than to be lost forever.

It is better to face God with humility than to be faced with his wrath.

It is better to receive a spiritual gift that will last
forever versus a natural that will fade away.

It is better to be among the living than to live with the dead.

These are just some of the things why it is better
to live for God and not the devil.

Paint Your Future
with
Practical Points for Reflection

List three words that best describe what this poem means to your life.

1. _____.

2. _____.

3. _____.

After reading this poem, list three characteristics you want to change for the better.

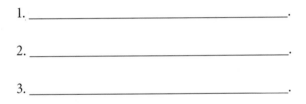

1. _____.

2. _____.

3. _____.

Take- Action

Do things that will shape your future.

1. Do not put off today for tomorrow.
2. Listen to wise men and women.
3. Make your life goals a priority.
4. Set a date to complete a task.
5. Have a mind to grow and stop settling for less.
6. Start small, then increase.

Romans 8:28
"And we know that all things work together for good to them that love God,
to them who are the called according to his purpose."

Rather Be

Would you rather be God's love child than a rich man greedy child?

Rather be humble in spirit than be bold in pride of life.

Rather be found in Christ than be lost in this world.

Would you rather be fighting for eternal life now than to receive temporary?

rewards now?

Rather love God's people than being hated by worldly people.

Rather strive for heavenly things than to go
after things that, only last for a moment.

Would you rather spend time with Jesus than
to spend your time on worthless living?

Rather be faithful to Jesus than be loyal to a man with drastic results.

Rather be dead in Christ than be alive in hell.

Would you rather receive the trophy of eternal life than to receive a gold statue?

that has no life?

We should seek to be alive in Jesus Christ.

Paint Your Future
with
Practical Points for Reflection

List three words that best describe what this poem means to your life.

1. _____.

2. _____.

3. _____.

After reading this poem, list three characteristics you want to change for the better.

1. _____.

2. _____.

3. _____.

Take-Action
Do things that will shape your future.

1. Do not put off today for tomorrow.
2. Listen to wise men and women.
3. Make your life goals a priority.
4. Set a date to complete a task.
5. Have a mind to grow and stop settling for less.
6. Start small, then increase.

2 Corinthians 3:6
"Who also hath made us able ministers of the new testament;
not of the letter, but of the spirit: for the letter killeth, but the spirit giveth life."

Journey to The Well

Every day we should have a journey,

to the well of everlasting love.

Sometimes our journey to the well of unspeakable

joy is cut off by evildoers.

Everywhere we go, we are looking for the journey,

to the well of everlasting peace.

Everybody whom we meet we should tell them,

about our journey to the well of everlasting goodness.

Journey to the well of true gentleness

is only found in Jesus Christ.

Let nothing keep you from abiding in Jesus's meekness.

Journey to the well of unmovable faith is,

worth living to please God.

A journey to the well of long-suffering is to be shared,

by all men and women of God.

Journey to the well of temperance is maintained,

only through the Holy Spirit.

Saints of God spread the fruit of the spirit,

when you are on your

journey to the well.

Paint Your Future
with
Practical Points for Reflection

List three words that best describe what this poem means to your life.

1. _____.

2. _____.

3. _____.

After reading this poem, list three characteristics you want to change for the better.

1. _____.

2. _____.

3. _____.

Take-Action
Do things that will shape your future.

1. Do not put off today for tomorrow.
2. Listen to wise men and women.
3. Make your life goals a priority.
4. Set a date to complete a task.
5. Have a mind to grow and stop settling for less.
6. Start small, then increase.

Psalms 121:8
The LORD shall preserve thy going out and
thy coming in from this time forth, and even for evermore.

Make Me Over

The Lord Jesus is making His people over by faith.

The Lord is making His children over by freeing them
from the social diseases of this world.

Jesus is forever making God's sons and daughters
over with kingdom, thinking.

The Lord make us over so he can take control
of our spiritual and natural lives.

It is Jesus's love that makes us over so we can love one another,

and be obedient to God and his ordain leadership.

The Lord is making us over so the devil
will not steal what, the Lord has for His people.

To receive salvation in Jesus Christ, we must be made over,

and believe he died and rose on the third day.

We must be made over to witness to the lost
and to encourage, those who are in the faith.

The Lord is making His people over so they can have victory

living their Christian life.

Lord, make us over so you can defeat the plan the devil has for us.

Paint Your Future
with
Practical Points for Reflection

List three words that best describe what this poem means to your life.

     1. _____.

     2. _____.

     3. _____.

After reading this poem, list three characteristics you want to change for the better.

     1. _____.

     2. _____.

     3. _____.

Take-Action
Do things that will shape your future.

1. Do not put off today for tomorrow.
2. Listen to wise men and women.
3. Make your life goals a priority.
4. Set a date to complete a task.
5. Have a mind to grow and stop settling for less.
6. Start small, then increase.

2 Corinthians 5:17
"Therefore, if any man be in Christ, he is a new creature:
old things are passed away; behold, all things are become new."

Nowhere

You have a lot of money, yet you are nowhere.

You have a lot of material goods, yet you are nowhere.

You have many friends, yet you are nowhere.

You have gold around your neck, arms,

and fingers, yet you are nowhere.

You have received several college degrees,

yet you are nowhere.

You have set world records, yet you are nowhere.

You are a philanthropist, yet you are nowhere.

These are just some of the things that will,

cause us to be nowhere.

The only time anyone gets anywhere is when,

they are in Jesus Christ.

It is good for us to be a part of the dead in

Christ than to be alive,

nowhere.

Paint Your Future
with
Practical Points for Reflection

List three words that best describe what this poem means to your life.

1. _____.

2. _____.

3. _____.

After reading this poem, list three characteristics you want to change for the better.

1. _____.

2. _____.

3. _____.

Take-Action

Do things that will shape your future.

1. Do not put off today for tomorrow.
2. Listen to wise men and women.
3. Make your life goals a priority.
4. Set a date to complete a task.
5. Have a mind to grow and stop settling for less.
6. Start small, then increase.

Mark 8:36
"For what shall it profit a man,
if he shall gain the whole world, and lose his own soul?"

No Bread

We come to church and leave with no bread.

Without bread in a Christian's life,
we cannot handle the pressures of life.

No bread means no life in Jesus Christ.

No bread causes Christians to be tempted by the devil.

No bread leaves Christians uncaring and unloving about each other.

No bread brings about false doctrine.

Without the anointed bread of Jesus Christ,
we will not be successful, at doing kingdom work.

People who live their lives without the bread of Jesus will die spiritually.

No bread in our lives will allow situations in our lives to doubt Jesus.

No bread will cause us to think things of this world instead,

of thinking on things of Heaven.

No bread reduces your faith in Jesus Christ.

Without the bread of Jesus Christ, we begin to serve two masters.

Without faith in Jesus Christ and His words,

Christians will live a life of no bread.

Paint Your Future
with
Practical Points for Reflection

List three words that best describe what this poem means to your life.

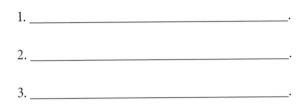

1. _____.

2. _____.

3. _____.

After reading this poem, list three characteristics you want to change for the better.

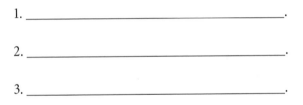

1. _____.

2. _____.

3. _____.

Take-Action
Do things that will shape your future.

1. Do not put off today for tomorrow.
2. Listen to wise men and women.
3. Make your life goals a priority.
4. Set a date to complete a task.
5. Have a mind to grow and stop settling for less.
6. Start small, then increase.

Matthew 4:4
"But he answered and said, It is written, Man shall not live by bread alone,
but by every word that proceedeth out of the mouth of God."

Our Place

Our place in Jesus Christ is to be in His word.

To take our faith to another level.

To operate through the Holy Spirit.

To love Him and His people unconditionally.

To live a life, he preordained for us to live,

before we were born.

To believe in the promises he gave to the church.

To obey his every commandment.

To worship Him in truth and spirit.

To listen to His apostles, prophets, evangelists,

preachers, and teachers.

To receive salvation and tell someone about it.

To witness to the lost.

Our place in Jesus should be as transparent as the blue water

ocean, and as bright as the morning star.

Paint Your Future
with
Practical Points for Reflection

List three words that best describe what this poem means to your life.

1. _____.

2. _____.

3. _____.

After reading this poem, list three characteristics you want to change for the better.

1. _____.

2. _____.

3. _____.

Take- Action

Do things that will shape your future.

1. Do not put off today for tomorrow.
2. Listen to wise men and women.
3. Make your life goals a priority.
4. Set a date to complete a task.
5. Have a mind to grow and stop settling for less.
6. Start small, then increase.

Romans 14:8
"For whether we live, we live unto the Lord; and whether we die,
we die unto the Lord: whether we live therefore, or die, we are the Lord's."

Peculiar People

Children of God are set apart to be peculiar people.

Peculiar people are not doomed to disease, poverty, and sins of this world.

Peculiar people are the light of the world to be seen by everyone.

Peculiar people say yes to God's will and way.

Peculiar people follow peace and are activated by their faith.

Peculiar people receive the promises God has for His people.

Peculiar people want nothing, and God keeps them from evil.

Peculiar people live to please God and his people.

Peculiar people live a long life and live to see their young grow old.

Peculiar people are God's pride and joy for now and forever.

Peculiar people live to tell the lost that God loves them and

He is a keeper of His promises.

Peculiar people are a unique group of people who is full,

of God's grace and love.

Paint Your Future
with
Practical Points for Reflection

List three words that best describe what this poem means to your life.

1. _____.

2. _____.

3. _____.

After reading this poem, list three characteristics you want to change for the better.

1. _____.

2. _____.

3. _____.

Take -Action

Do things that will shape your future.

1. Do not put off today for tomorrow.
2. Listen to wise men and women.
3. Make your life goals a priority.
4. Set a date to complete a task.
5. Have a mind to grow and stop settling for less.
6. Start small, then increase.

1 Peter 2:9

"But ye *are* a chosen generation, a royal priesthood,
a holy nation, a peculiar people; that ye should shew forth the praises
of him who hath called you out of darkness into his marvelous light:"

Pray

Pray in faith will move a still mountain.

Pray power is a billion-man army.

Pray releases joy and peace in a perilous life.

Pray is the active agent in victory and the antidote against defeat.

Pray will reach Heaven like love touching a weary heart.

Pray will cast out fear and shed light on a crying tear.

Pray will give you confidence when all odds are against you.

Pray gives hope in the life to come.

Pray is the answer to all things and opens the door to everything.

Pray will reshape the heart and mind to be in harmony with God.

Pray reaches out to the soul man like music reaches the heart of man.

Pray will draw Christians close to God like a magnet draws its object.

Pray is like a river forever flowing.

Pray can be as long as a debate or as short as a size one shoe.

Pray is not something we do momentarily,
but it is something, we live to do.

Paint Your Future
With
Practical Points for Reflection

List three words that best describe what this poem means to your life.

1. _____.

2. _____.

3. _____.

After reading this poem, list three characteristics you want to change for the better.

1. _____.

2. _____.

3. _____.

Take-Action

Do things that will shape your future.

1. Do not put off today for tomorrow.
2. Listen to wise men and women.
3. Make your life goals a priority.
4. Set a date to complete a task.
5. Have a mind to grow and stop settling for less.
6. Start small, then increase.

Philippians 4:6
"Be careful for nothing, but in everything by prayer and supplication
with thanksgiving, let your requests be made known unto God."

What Will It Take?

What will it take for you to believe Jesus is the Savior of the world?

What will it take to convince you that Jesus can do all things?

through your faith in Him?

What will it take for you to receive his gift of the Holy Spirit?

What will it take for you to live a righteous life?

What will it take for you to forgive your fellow man and yourself?

What will it take for you to receive the spiritual gifts God gave to the church?

What will it take for you to serve Jesus in spirit and truth?

What will it take for you to put away envy and strife you have against others?

What will it take for you to believe we are not serving God in vain?

What will it take for you to endure to the end
and reap the promises, God has for you,

People of God, what will it take?

It will take for us to endure until the end and be faithful until death.

Paint Your Future
with
Practical Points for Reflection

List three words that best describe what this poem means to your life.

1. _____.

2. _____.

3. _____.

After reading this poem, list three characteristics you want to change for the better.

1. _____.

2. _____.

3. _____.

Take-Action
Do things that will shape your future.

1. Do not put off today for tomorrow.
2. Listen to wise men and women.
3. Make your life goals a priority.
4. Set a date to complete a task.
5. Have a mind to grow and stop settling for less.
6. Start small, then increase.

Hebrews 11:6
"But without faith, it is impossible to please him:
for he that cometh to God must believe that he is,
and *that* he is a rewarder of them that diligently seek him."

Worship

Children of God worship whether they are happy or sad.

Saints of God worship Jesus through
their sickness and good health.

Children of God worship the Lord Jesus,
so he can take control over their mind, body, and soul.

Worshipping Jesus will allow God to destroy yokes
and tear down, strongholds in your life.

Children of God worship the Lord Jesus
to let the devil know we do not, belong to him.

Saints worship God to have the power to witness
to the lost and to encourage those in the faith,

Saints worship Jesus to be delivered from worldly things.

Children of God worship Jesus to let God know
how much, we love and adorn him.

Children of God who are sold out to Jesus will have a hard time finding,

something on earth that will take the place
of praising and worshipping God.

Saints worship God to have an abundant life now,

and eternal life forever.

Paint Your Future
with
Practical Points for Reflection

List three words that best describe what this poem means to your life.

1. _____.

2. _____.

3. _____.

After reading this poem, list three characteristics you want to change for the better.

1. _____.

2. _____.

3. _____.

Take-Action

Do things that will shape your future.

1. Do not put off today for tomorrow.
2. Listen to wise men and women.
3. Make your life goals a priority.
4. Set a date to complete a task.
5. Have a mind to grow and stop settling for less.
6. Start small, then increase.

John 4:24
"God *is* a Spirit: and they that worship him must
worship him in spirit and in truth."

Doing It on Purpose

Are we laser-focused on our purpose today?

To witness to your family members,

to show kindness, love, and forgiveness
to those who do not deserve it.

To live by faith and trust God with your life.

To use your talents of singing, playing musical instruments,

rapping, writing,

artwork, or dancing to please God.

To have better church attendance.

To join a ministry and do kingdom work.

To invite your friends to church.

To have a life ordained by God.

To serve God with gladness and not resentment.

To live by faith and not by chance.

If you want your heart to be right before God,

do things on purpose.

Paint Your Future
with
Practical Points for Reflection

List three words that best describe what this poem means to your life.

1. _____.

2. _____.

3. _____.

After reading this poem, list three characteristics you want to change for the better.

1. _____.

2. _____.

3. _____.

Take-Action
Do things that will shape your future.

1. Do not put off today for tomorrow.
2. Listen to wise men and women.
3. Make your life goals a priority.
4. Set a date to complete a task.
5. Have a mind to grow and stop settling for less.
6. Start small, then increase.

Colossians 3:23-24
"And whatever you do, do it heartily, as to the Lord and not to men,
knowing that from the Lord you will receive the reward of the inheritance;
for you serve the Lord Christ."

POEMS OF JESUS'S ATTRIBUTES

Jesus: Who is he?

Jesus is the one who created heaven, earth,
and everything that, lives in it.

Jesus is the one who was born to take away the sins of the world.

Jesus is the one who walks among the king, queens, and religious leaders.

Jesus is the one who performed miracles, so the blind can see, the mute can

speak, the deaf can hear, and the disabled person can walk.

Jesus is the one who is known as the prophet, evangelist, preacher,

teachers, forgiver of sin, healer, and friend.

Jesus is the one who created discipleship.

Jesus is the one who died on the cross at Calvary.

Jesus is the one who conquers sin, death, and grave.

Jesus is God the Father, God the Son, and God the Holy Spirit.

Jesus is the one who gave Apostle Peter the keys to the church.

Jesus is the one who gave us the gift of salvation.

Jesus is the one who calls apostle, prophet, evangelist, preacher

and teacher for the edification and upkeep of the church.

When someone asks you, who is Jesus think about these things?

Paint Your Future
with
Practical Points for Reflection

List three words that best describe what this poem means to your life.

1. _____.

2. _____.

3. _____.

After reading this poem, list three characteristics you want to change for the better.

1. _____.

2. _____.

3. _____.

Take-Action
Do things that will shape your future.

1. Do not put off today for tomorrow.
2. Listen to wise men and women.
3. Make your life goals a priority.
4. Set a date to complete a task.
5. Have a mind to grow and stop settling for less.
6. Start small, then increase.

John 11:25
"Jesus said unto her, I am the resurrection, and the life:
he that believeth in me, though he were dead, yet shall he live:"

Jesus: A Friend

He is a friend you can talk to in the morning and throughout the day.

A friend who can change your feelings of sorrow
to happiness, love, joy, and peace.

A friend you can count on because he is always there
when you need him.

He is a friend who knows your heart
like a road map to the Promise Land.

He is the kind of friend who keeps his promises.

A friend who will keep you safe from all harm and danger.

A friend who delights in your obedient to God's laws.

A friend who wants you to have blessings instead of curses.

He is a friend that will supply all your needs.

A friend who will stand by you,

when family and friends deny you.

He is a friend who can set you free from earthly sins.

He is a friend who knows your beginning and your end.

Paint Your Future
with
Practical Points for Reflection

List three words that best describe what this poem means to your life.

1. _____.

2. _____.

3. _____.

After reading this poem, list three characteristics you want to change for the better.

1. _____.

2. _____.

3. _____.

Take-Action
Do things that will shape your future.

1. Do not put off today for tomorrow.
2. Listen to wise men and women.
3. Make your life goals a priority.
4. Set a date to complete a task.
5. Have a mind to grow and stop settling for less.
6. Start small, then increase.

John 15:13
"Greater love hath no man than this,
that a man lay down his life for his friends."

Jesus: The Redeemer

A redeemer who can turn your stormy day into a sunny day.

A redeemer who can change your life from a cold-blooded killer

To someone who mentors wayward teenagers.

A redeemer who can mold his children
from an imperfect life to a life of perfection.

A redeemer who can shape your character
from a brawling fighter, to a humble giant.

He is a kind of redeemer who leaves his people breathless
like a runner, puffing for air.

A redeemer who can rescue you from a shipwrecked life
to a life that, is focused on doing the will of God.

He is a redeemer who can reconcile you back
to God like a mother, who takes back a lost child.

A redeemer who can give his children prosperity
and make, the evil one's poor.

He is a redeemer that can take back what the devil stole from you.

A redeemer who never regrets put restores what was lost.

Paint Your Future
with
Practical Points for Reflection

List three words that best describe what this poem means to your life.

1. _____.

2. _____.

3. _____.

After reading this poem, list three characteristics you want to change for the better.

1. _____.

2. _____.

3. _____.

Take-Action
Do things that will shape your future.

1. Do not put off today for tomorrow.
2. Listen to wise men and women.
3. Make your life goals a priority.
4. Set a date to complete a task.
5. Have a mind to grow and stop settling for less.
6. Start small, then increase.

John 1:29
"The next day John seeth Jesus coming unto him,
and saith, Behold the Lamb of God, which taketh away the sin of the world."

Jesus: No Ordinary God

There is no other God that can save you from your sins except Jesus.

No ordinary God can heal you from the inside out like Jesus.

No other God can deliver you from
the ungodly things of this world, but Jesus.

No ordinary God can give you his spirit besides Jesus.

There is no other God on earth that can
supply all your needs, accept Jesus.

No other God can give you eternal life other than Jesus.

No other God can give you peace now and forever than Jesus.

No other God can love you unconditionally but Jesus.

No other God can be all-powerful, all-knowing,
and everywhere, besides Jesus.

There is no other god who has a prepared place for a

prepared people but Jesus.

Jesus truly is No Ordinary God.

Paint Your Future
with
Practical Points for Reflection

List three words that best describe what this poem means to your life.

1. _____.

2. _____.

3. _____.

After reading this poem, list three characteristics you want to change for the better.

1. _____.

2. _____.

3. _____.

Take-Action
Do things that will shape your future.

1. Do not put off today for tomorrow.
2. Listen to wise men and women.
3. Make your life goals a priority.
4. Set a date to complete a task.
5. Have a mind to grow and stop settling for less.
6. Start small, then increase.

Romans 1:20
"For the invisible things of him from the creation of the world are clearly seen,
being understood by the things that are made, even his eternal power and Godhead;
so that they are without excuse:"

Jesus: He's a Great God

There is no other God compared to our great God.

There is no other God who can lift your
burdens of sin like our great God.

There is no other God who can deliver you from the sin-sick,

diseases of this world like our great God.

No one can save you from eternal
damnation but our, great God.

No one on earth is more powerful than our great God.

Our great God is the only creator of Heaven and earth.

Our great God is the one who can sustain life and he can take life.

He is the only God who gave his disciples
the words of life found, in the Bible.

No one can give peace to a lost soul like our great God.

No other God can endure to the end
and suffers patiently, like our great God.

Our great God is eternal.

Who would not want to serve a God who can do everything?

Jesus is a great God.

Paint Your Future
with
Practical Points for Reflection

List three words that best describe what this poem means to your life.

1. _____.

2. _____.

3. _____.

After reading this poem, list three characteristics you want to change for the better.

1. _____.

2. _____.

3. _____.

Take-Action
Do things that will shape your future.

1. Do not put off today for tomorrow.
2. Listen to wise men and women.
3. Make your life goals a priority.
4. Set a date to complete a task.
5. Have a mind to grow and stop settling for less.
6. Start small, then increase.

Nahum 1:7
"The LORD *is* good, a strong hold in the day of trouble;
and he knoweth them that trust in him."

Jesus: The Bible

The Bible is the only book on planet earth,

that has survived over 2000 years.

The Bible is the only divine book,

that has a roadmap for your earthly

and eternal lives.

God's code of justice

Is found in the Bible.

Saints of God can understand God's gift,

of the Holy Spirit by reading the Bible.

The Bible is the only book that was,

written to stir the emotions,

of sinners and saints to do God's will

and repent from their sins.

God defeated the devil and wrote it all in the Bible.

When you need God to go and read his Bible.

What an awesome God we serve reincarnate as a man, so

we can see, hear, feel, and taste the Bible.

Paint Your Future
with
Practical Points for Reflection

List three words that best describe what this poem means to your life.

1. _____.

2. _____.

3. _____.

After reading this poem, list three characteristics you want to change for the better.

1. _____.

2. _____.

3. _____.

Take-Action

Do things that will shape your future.

1. Do not put off today for tomorrow.
2. Listen to wise men and women.
3. Make your life goals a priority.
4. Set a date to complete a task.
5. Have a mind to grow and stop settling for less.
6. Start small, then increase.

Matthew 4:4
"But he answered and said, It is written, Man shall not live by bread alone,
but by every word that proceedeth out of the mouth of God."

Jesus: The Heart Fixer

When you are low and lonely, Jesus becomes your heart fixer.

Trouble has entered your life, and you are sick with grief,

know that Jesus is your heart fixer.

Friends, family, and coworkers criticize and belittle you,
know that, Jesus is your heart fixer.

People slander your name because they are jealous of you,
but remember, Jesus is your heart fixer.

Your sins have weighed you down, and you ask Jesus
for forgiveness, so he can be your heart fixer.

You are lost and in despair, but you know Jesus is your heart fixer.

Different experiences in your life have left you disappointed,

but you know Jesus is your heart fixer.

You have failed at achieving the goals you wanted to happen in

your life, yet you know Jesus is your heart fixer.

Your family members and friends are decease,

yet you know Jesus is a heart fixer.

You lost your job and your car is repossessed,

your girlfriend gave you a

Dear John's letter, yet you know Jesus is your heart fixer.

No matter what is going on in your life,

reminded yourself,

Jesus is your heart fixer.

Paint Your Future
with
Practical Points for Reflection

List three words that best describe what this poem means to your life.

1. _____.

2. _____.

3. _____.

After reading this poem, list three characteristics you want to change for the better.

1. _____.

2. _____.

3. _____.

Take-Action
Do things that will shape your future.

1. Do not put off today for tomorrow.
2. Listen to wise men and women.
3. Make your life goals a priority.
4. Set a date to complete a task.
5. Have a mind to grow and stop settling for less.
6. Start small, then increase.

Psalms 147:3
"He heals the broken in heart and binds up their wounds."

POEMS OF CELEBRATION

Glad

Are you Glad God gave us a choice to choose,

between Him or the world?

A choice to choose a God who can do all things,

a God who can deliver us,

from every problem life gives to us.

Are you glad God is able to give life and conquer death?

a God who can us from our sins,

a God who can turn darkness into light,

a God who can turn a stony heart into

a heart of flesh.

Are you glad Jesus is who he says he is, the Savior of the world?

Jesus allowed his apostles to write the living word,

so we can live by His statutes.

Are you glad God forgave us of our sins through his son Jesus?

and gave us eternal life.

People of God, are you glad?

Paint Your Future
with
Practical Points for Reflection

List three words that best describe what this poem means to your life.

1. _____.

2. _____.

3. _____.

After reading this poem, list three characteristics you want to change for the better.

1. _____.

2. _____.

3. _____.

Take-Action
Do things that will shape your future.

1. Do not put off today for tomorrow.
2. Listen to wise men and women.
3. Make your life goals a priority.
4. Set a date to complete a task.
5. Have a mind to grow and stop settling for less.
6. Start small, then increase.

Psalms 126:3
"The LORD hath done great things for us; whereof we are glad."

Freedom

Loving Jesus will give you a sense of freedom,

no one can take from you.

If people only knew how real Jesus is, they too can,

experience real freedom.

You are no longer bonded to sin if,

you possess Jesus's freedom,

To receive freedom in Jesus Christ,

you have to say yes to

His will and His way.

Jesus's love is freedom.

You think the 4th of July is a celebration of freedom,

Wait until you receive the gift of the Holy Spirit,

and live a life of

everlasting freedom.

Paint Your Future
with
Practical Points for Reflection

List three words that best describe what this poem means to your life.

1. _____.

2. _____.

3. _____.

After reading this poem, list three characteristics you want to change for the better.

1. _____.

2. _____.

3. _____.

Take-Action
Do things that will shape your future.

1. Do not put off today for tomorrow.
2. Listen to wise men and women.
3. Make your life goals a priority.
4. Set a date to complete a task.
5. Have a mind to grow and stop settling for less.
6. Start small, then increase.

2 Corinthians 3:17
"Now the Lord is that Spirit: and where the Spirit of the Lord is, there is liberty."

He Lives

He lives in your heart.

He lives in every part of your body.

He lives in you so you can receive His blessings.

He lives to show the devil he is defeated.

He lives so you can delight in His principles.

He lives so you can walk in the light.

He lives today, tomorrow, and forever.

He lives so you can be His witness to a dying world.

He lives so you can be magnifying through your faith in him.

He lives to give the earth and heaven life.

He lives to save souls.

He lives so you can have eternal life.

He lives never to be forgotten.

He lives just for you and me.

Paint Your Future
with
Practical Points for Reflection

List three words that best describe what this poem means to your life.

1. _____.

2. _____.

3. _____.

After reading this poem, list three characteristics you want to change for the better.

1. _____.

2. _____.

3. _____.

Take-Action

Do things that will shape your future.

1. Do not put off today for tomorrow.
2. Listen to wise men and women.
3. Make your life goals a priority.
4. Set a date to complete a task.
5. Have a mind to grow and stop settling for less.
6. Start small, then increase.

Revelation 1:18
"I am he that liveth, and was dead; and, behold, I am alive for evermore, Amen; and have the keys of hell and of death."

Contentment

To be content, you Jesus is the son of God,
who died on the cross for all humankind.

You are content with the Apostle Doctrine,

and your Christian faith.

Your contentment in Jesus allows you to be satisfied with the
and the spiritual gift or gifts God has given to you.

Your contentment in Jesus has allowed you to trust God with your life.

You are content knowing God will supply all your needs.

Contentment in Jesus helps you
to apply his word in your, everyday life living.

Contentment in Jesus brings about the blessings

God has for each of us.

Contentment is to know God is in control of your

life through His Holy Spirit.

After living, listening, and witnessing about the true religion,

of God, you will experience contentment no one can give you.

Live for God and be content today and forever.

Paint Your Future
with
Practical Points for Reflection

List three words that best describe what this poem means to your life.

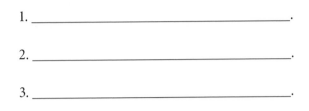

1. _____.

2. _____.

3. _____.

After reading this poem, list three characteristics you want to change for the better.

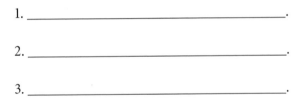

1. _____.

2. _____.

3. _____.

Take-Action
Do things that will shape your future.

1. Do not put off today for tomorrow.
2. Listen to wise men and women.
3. Make your life goals a priority.
4. Set a date to complete a task.
5. Have a mind to grow and stop settling for less.
6. Start small, then increase.

1 Timothy 6:6
"But godliness with contentment is great gain."

Gifts to Glorify God

God gives His children gifts so they can,

win souls for his kingdom.

God gives us abilities that will last a lifetime.

It is the Holy Spirit that unleashes the hidden gifts within us.

Without the wisdom and power of God's word,
our talents would be buried.

It is the anointing of the Holy Spirit that active our gifts,

to bring lost souls to God.

All of God's children have gifts to do kingdom work.

Our gifts are meant to glorify God and not ourselves.

Gifts to heal the sick, to bring sight to the blind, to unstopped,

deaf ears, the limb will walk, and the speechless will speak.

Let us all use our God-given gifts to glorify God and not ourselves.

Paint Your Future
with
Practical Points for Reflection

List three words that best describe what this poem means to your life.

1. _____.

2. _____.

3. _____.

After reading this poem, list three characteristics you want to change for the better.

1. _____.

2. _____.

3. _____.

Take-Action
Do things that will shape your future.

1. Do not put off today for tomorrow.
2. Listen to wise men and women.
3. Make your life goals a priority.
4. Set a date to complete a task.
5. Have a mind to grow and stop settling for less.
6. Start small, then increase.

1 Peter 4:10
As every man hath received the gift,
even so, minister the same one to another,
as good stewards of the manifold grace of God.

Paradise

It is written in the Bible that paradise does exist for those who

believe Jesus is the Savior of the world.

If your name is written in the Book of Life,
you are going to paradise.

Paradise now on earth is the love, joy, peace,
and Jesus's forgiveness of our sins.

A paradise is a prepared place for a prepared people.

Paradise is for now and forever.

Paradise is waiting to be filled with God's people.

Paradise is not for those who lust after their flesh,

but for them who glorify God in their spirit.

Paint Your Future
with
Practical Points for Reflection

List three words that best describe what this poem means to your life.

1. _____.

2. _____.

3. _____.

After reading this poem, list three characteristics you want to change for the better.

1. _____.

2. _____.

3. _____.

Take-Action

Do things that will shape your future.

1. Do not put off today for tomorrow.
2. Listen to wise men and women.
3. Make your life goals a priority.
4. Set a date to complete a task.
5. Have a mind to grow and stop settling for less.
6. Start small, then increase.

Psalms 37:29
"The righteous shall inherit the land and dwell therein forever."

God's Talent

God gives some of us one talent and others many talents.

Our talents come from God, and it is only
revealed to us through, his Holy Spirit.

God's talent is supernatural, and it destroys sin from its roots.

Without the Holy Spirit, wisdom, and power of God's word

our talents would be buried.

It is the Holy Spirit who anoints our talent to do God's will.

The Holy Spirit wants believers to use their talent
or talents to empower God's children.

It is God's talent or talents that change the lives of sinners and

encourage the faithful to serve God until death.

Extraordinary talents for ordinary people only come from God.

Paint Your Future
with
Practical Points for Reflection

List three words that best describe what this poem means to your life.

1. _____.

2. _____.

3. _____.

After reading this poem, list three characteristics you want to change for the better.

1. _____.

2. _____.

3. _____.

Take-Action
Do things that will shape your future.

1. Do not put off today for tomorrow.
2. Listen to wise men and women.
3. Make your life goals a priority.
4. Set a date to complete a task.
5. Have a mind to grow and stop settling for less.
6. Start small, then increase.

Ephesians 2:10
"For we are his workmanship, created in Christ Jesus unto good works,
which God hath before ordained that we should walk in them."

Hope

Hope in Jesus Christ is like seeing a miracle before your eyes.

It brings believers closer to the all-powerful, all-knowing

and everywhere kind of God.

It builds our faith to know that one day God's children

will be with him for eternity.

Hope in Jesus Christ help believers to be at peace with themselves and others.

Hope helps Christians to be free of sin.

Hope allows believers to stay on the path of righteousness.

Hope helps Christians to obey God's commandments.

Hope in Jesus Christ help believers to stay pure and humble before God.

Hope allows the children of God to escape spiritual death.

Hope in Jesus Christ keeps Christians from falling into despair.

Hope gives saints a reason to endure faith until death.

Hope, what a beautiful thought to live by.

Paint Your Future
with
Practical Points for Reflection

List three words that best describe what this poem means to your life.

1. _____.

2. _____.

3. _____.

After reading this poem, list three characteristics you want to change for the better.

1. _____.

2. _____.

3. _____.

Take-Action
Do things that will shape your future.

1. Do not put off today for tomorrow.
2. Listen to wise men and women.
3. Make your life goals a priority.
4. Set a date to complete a task.
5. Have a mind to grow and stop settling for less.
6. Start small, then increase.

Psalms 33:18
"Behold, the eye of the LORD *is* upon them that fear him,
upon them that hope in his mercy."

Grateful

Are you grateful to be among believers in Jesus Christ?

Grateful to know we are few, yet our love
for one another is immeasurable.

Grateful to be among the saints who are not a shame to worship,

sing, dance, and shout praises to our God.

Grateful to see your brothers and sisters witnessing about the

saving grace of our Lord and Savior Jesus Christ.

Grateful to have a mind to serve Jesus Christ
rather than the things of this world.

Grateful for the pastors and ministers who are teaching and

preaching the true words of God found in the Bible.

Grateful to see the saints standing on the promises of God.

Grateful to be a part of the royal family.

Grateful for the food you eat, the clothes you wear,
and the shoes on your feet.

Grateful for your natural family and church family.

No matter what is going on in your life, you know it is God's grace

and mercy that will keep you until death.

These are just some of the reasons why we should be grateful.

Paint Your Future
with
Practical Points for Reflection

List three words that best describe what this poem means to your life.

1. _____.

2. _____.

3. _____.

After reading this poem, list three characteristics you want to change for the better.

1. _____.

2. _____.

3. _____.

Take-Action
Do things that will shape your future.

1. Do not put off today for tomorrow.
2. Listen to wise men and women.
3. Make your life goals a priority.
4. Set a date to complete a task.
5. Have a mind to grow and stop settling for less.
6. Start small, then increase.

1 Thessalonians 5:16-18
Rejoice evermore. Pray without ceasing.
In everything give thanks, for this is the will of God
in Christ Jesus concerning you.

Shout Jesus

When you are thinking about the goodness of God, shout Jesus.

When Jesus has brought you through a test or a storm, shout Jesus.

When family and friends fail, you shout Jesus.

When God gives you his spirit, shout Jesus.

When you are blessed with health and wealth, shout Jesus.

When God gives you your ministry, shout Jesus.

When you witness to God's people, shout Jesus.

When you are in despair, shout Jesus.

When you are lost, shout Jesus.

When you need traveling mercy, shout Jesus.

When death strikes, your family shouts Jesus.

When you are sick, shout Jesus.

When life becomes unbearable, shout Jesus.

No matter what is going on in your life, shout Jesus and receive

the victory God has for your life.

Paint Your Future
with
Practical Points for Reflection

List three words that best describe what this poem means to your life.

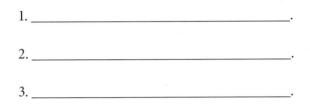

1. _____.

2. _____.

3. _____.

After reading this poem, list three characteristics you want to change for the better.

1. _____.

2. _____.

3. _____.

Take-Action
Do things that will shape your future.

1. Do not put off today for tomorrow.
2. Listen to wise men and women.
3. Make your life goals a priority.
4. Set a date to complete a task.
5. Have a mind to grow and stop settling for less.
6. Start small, then increase.

Psalms 98:4
Make a joyful noise unto the LORD, all the earth:
make a loud noise, and rejoice, and sing praise.

KISS

Kiss the life of Jesus Christ.
Kiss Jesus's love, joy, and peace for your life.
Kiss Jesus's prophets, teachers, and preachers to help
guide you to God.
Kiss Jesus healing power.
Kiss Jesus everlasting love.
Kiss Jesus salvation in the Holy Ghost
Kiss Jesus greatness.
Kiss Jesus living words.
Kiss Jesus church.
Kiss Jesus music.
Kiss Jesus's hope on the cross.
Kiss Jesus presences now and forever.
Kiss Jesus's mercy and grace.
Kiss Jesus's spirit and truth.
Kiss the Savior Jesus Christ and live forever.
Kiss your way straight into heaven.

Paint Your Future
with
Practical Points for Reflection

List three words that best describe what this poem means to your life.

1. _____.

2. _____.

3. _____.

After reading this poem, list three characteristics you want to change for the better.

1. _____.

2. _____.

3. _____.

Take-Action
Do things that will shape your future.

1. Do not put off today for tomorrow.
2. Listen to wise men and women.
3. Make your life goals a priority.
4. Set a date to complete a task.
5. Have a mind to grow and stop settling for less.
6. Start small, then increase.

Psalm 85:10
Mercy and truth are met together, righteousness
and peace have kissed each other.

Love

Jesus's love is like a forest on fire.

It is a love that cannot be explained or described.

It is a love that runs deep as the Red Sea and as high

as Mount Everest.

It is a love that tastes better than Butter Pecan ice cream.

It is a love that is wider than all

college football fields.

It is a love that can solve any problem, sickness,

and sorrow you may have.

Jesus's love is like a million hugs and kisses.

Jesus' love is more frequent than a cruise ship sail, and

more powerful than a rocket to the moon.

Jesus's love is an endless song and an everlasting dance.

Paint Your Future
with
Practical Points for Reflection

List three words that best describe what this poem means to your life.

1. _____.

2. _____.

3. _____.

After reading this poem, list three characteristics you want to change for the better.

1. _____.

2. _____.

3. _____.

Take-Action
Do things that will shape your future.

1. Do not put off today for tomorrow.
2. Listen to wise men and women.
3. Make your life goals a priority.
4. Set a date to complete a task.
5. Have a mind to grow and stop settling for less.
6. Start small, then increase.

John 3:16
"For God so loved the world, that he gave his only begotten Son,
that whosoever believeth in him should not perish but have everlasting life."

Open Door

Jesus can open the door of a close heart that has
been shut by fear.
Jesus has opened the doors of salvation and
everlasting peace for those who believe he is the son of God.
Jesus's doors of health, sound mind, and wealth come
to those who trust Jesus as their personal
Lord and Savior.
Jesus will open the door for your next job promotion.
Jesus has opened his door so that we can overcome sin.
Jesus open doors are not just earthly treasures but are
heavenly blessings.
Jesus opens his door to fellowship and cast out division.
Jesus's door can deliver you from any bondage
that has entered into your life.
Jesus will open his door so that you can receive the
gift of the Holy Spirit.
Jesus's door is open to backsliders.
Jesus is the only one who can get you through
a closed door to an open door.

Paint Your Future
with
Practical Points for Reflection

List three words that best describe what this poem means to your life.

1. _____.

2. _____.

3. _____.

After reading this poem, list three characteristics you want to change for the better.

1. _____.

2. _____.

3. _____.

Take-Action

Do things that will shape your future.

1. Do not put off today for tomorrow.
2. Listen to wise men and women.
3. Make your life goals a priority.
4. Set a date to complete a task.
5. Have a mind to grow and stop settling for less.
6. Start small, then increase.

Isaiah 22:22
"And the key of the house of David will I lay upon his shoulder;
so, he shall open, and none shall shut; and he shall shut, and none shall open."

God's Calling You

You want to be a recording artist, but God
has called you to preach the Gospel.

A calling to seek after lost souls and
encourage others to stay in the faith.

A calling that will impact your family,
friends, communities, and society at large.

A calling that will allow you to live a life with vision and purpose.

A calling that esteems your self-worth because
you know God has a plan for your life.

It is a calling that does not qualify you
by your sex, height, race, weight, social status,

financial status, and political view, but a calling
that God ordains you to do Kingdom work.

A calling that can defeat your enemies and have your
bullies running in another direction.

A calling that will never leave you alone because
Jesus is there to help you through the storms of life.

A calling that will allow you to hide God's word
in your heart so you will know his desires.

A calling for you to study your Bible so you
can bring others into the saving faith of Jesus.

A calling for you to use your gift or gifts to witness
to the lost and encourage others.

A calling to look for an opportunity to witness,
teach, preach, coach, and mentor others.

A calling that is designed especially for you.

God's calling you!

Paint Your Future
with
Practical Points for Reflection

List three words that best describe what this poem means to your life.

1. _____.

2. _____.

3. _____.

After reading this poem, list three characteristics you want to change for the better.

1. _____.

2. _____.

3. _____.

Take-Action
Do things that will shape your future.

1. Do not put off today for tomorrow.
2. Listen to wise men and women.
3. Make your life goals a priority.
4. Set a date to complete a task.
5. Have a mind to grow and stop settling for less.
6. Start small, then increase.

Romans 8:28
And we know that all things work together for good to them that love God,
to them who are the called according to his purpose.

POEMS OF OVERCOMING

The Only Way

The only way to reach God is through Jesus Christ.

The only way to love Jesus is through holiness.

The only way to think is to be Christ-like.

The only way to live is in righteousness.

The only way to treat your brethren is with love.

The only way to walk in Jesus is through obedience.

The only way to talk is of joy and peace.

The only way to salvation is in repentance.

The only way to succeed in Christ is to acknowledge

Him in all your ways.

The only way to heaven is to accept Jesus as your

Lord and Savior.

The only way to God is to obey his commandments

and live for eternity.

Jesus is the only way and one way only.

Paint Your Future
with
Practical Points for Reflection

List three words that best describe what this poem means to your life.

1. _____.

2. _____.

3. _____.

After reading this poem, list three characteristics you want to change for the better.

1. _____.

2. _____.

3. _____.

Take-Action

Do things that will shape your future.

1. Do not put off today for tomorrow.
2. Listen to wise men and women.
3. Make your life goals a priority.
4. Set a date to complete a task.
5. Have a mind to grow and stop settling for less.
6. Start small, then increase.

John 14:6
"Jesus saith unto him, I am the way, the truth,
and the life: no man cometh unto the Father, but by me."

Victory in Jesus

Victory in Jesus is like winning a 28 miles marathon race.
It is an everlasting event of love in motion.
A spirit that is not loud but humble.
A soul that is not filled with bullet holes of hate.
It is an attitude of care when others want to despair.
It is a life of hope that free you from the world streets
cover in dope.
Victory in Jesus will keep a song and praise in your heart and
on your lips.
It will give you a silent pray when everything else around you
seem unfair.
Victory in Jesus is not overdosing on money, food, and material
things of this world, but wanting spiritual growth and soberness
to fight Satan's buffet of sins.
Victory in Jesus is never lazy but always working
toward
an eternal trophy that will help you sing songs of victory,
so the devil will have none.

Paint Your Future
with
Practical Points for Reflection

List three words that best describe what this poem means to your life.

1. _____.

2. _____.

3. _____.

After reading this poem, list three characteristics you want to change for the better.

1. _____.

2. _____.

3. _____.

Take-Action
Do things that will shape your future.

1. Do not put off today for tomorrow.
2. Listen to wise men and women.
3. Make your life goals a priority.
4. Set a date to complete a task.
5. Have a mind to grow and stop settling for less.
6. Start small, then increase.

1 John 5:4
For whatsoever is born of God overcome the world:
and this is the victory that overcomes the world, even our faith.

Believe

Whatever is in your way, believe Jesus will move it out of your way.

People, places, and things that got you bonded
believe Jesus will move, them out of your way.

Sickness in your way; believe Jesus will heal it out of your way.

Enemies who are prosecuting you believe Jesus
will move them out of your way.

You are prosperous because you believe in Jesus.

Believers who are seeking the spirit of God believe Jesus will fill them.

Our faith in Jesus is high because of our relationship with him.

He is like a river that is forever flowing.

Believers know there is nothing Jesus can do.

Believe your children are saved, and Jesus will save them.

Believe in Jesus when everything is around you is falling apart.

Saint believe in your prayers, and Jesus will bless you.

Believe whatever situation you are in; Jesus will bring you out.

The part you believe is the part you will receive.

Children of God who believe in all of Jesus will receive all of Jesus.

People of God believe!

Paint Your Future
with
Practical Points for Reflection

List three words that best describe what this poem means to your life.

1. _____.

2. _____.

3. _____.

After reading this poem, list three characteristics you want to change for the better.

1. _____.

2. _____.

3. _____.

Take-Action
Do things that will shape your future.

1. Do not put off today for tomorrow.
2. Listen to wise men and women.
3. Make your life goals a priority.
4. Set a date to complete a task.
5. Have a mind to grow and stop settling for less.
6. Start small, then increase.

1 John 5:13
These things have I written unto you that believe on the name of the Son of God; that ye may know that ye have eternal life and that ye may believe on the name of the Son of God.

Holy Ghost Shoes

Your feet are beautiful when you put on your Holy Ghost shoes.

You walk swiftly to tell someone about the goodness of Jesus.

You rush to speak words of peace to those who are oppressed.

I got on Holy Ghost shoes.

You are walking in righteousness.

You speed walk to the Boys and Girl club so that you
can mentor others about the saving grace of God.

Your shoes transformed your character,
behavior, and attitude to be like Jesus.

I got on Holy Ghost shoes.

Your feet will move to spread the truth and not lies.

You are shifting in motion to bring joy and peace, not war.

You live to defeat evildoers.

I got on Holy Ghost shoes.

You tempted, yet you honor the words of God for your escape.

No matter the distance, you are faithful
to tell someone about the Gospel.

I got on Holy Ghost shoes.

Paint Your Future
with
Practical Points for Reflection

List three words that best describe what this poem means to your life.

1. _____.

2. _____.

3. _____.

After reading this poem, list three characteristics you want to change for the better.

1. _____.

2. _____.

3. _____.

Take-Action
Do things that will shape your future.

1. Do not put off today for tomorrow.
2. Listen to wise men and women.
3. Make your life goals a priority.
4. Set a date to complete a task.
5. Have a mind to grow and stop settling for less.
6. Start small, then increase.

1 Peter 1:15-16
But as he which hath called you is holy, so be ye holy in all manner of conversation;
Because it is written, Be ye holy; for I am holy.

Discipline or Regret

I would rather take the discipline of God than live a lifetime of regret.

Discipline in Christ is far better than the pain of regret.

Discipline today and regret forever.

God's love for us is expressed through discipline
to keep us from the tears of regret.

Discipline is what we need to head off the despair of regret.

Discipline allows us to make righteous choices
instead of making foolish choices.

Discipline brings about fear in God, and regret suffers long.

Discipline honor's God's incredible power,
and regret gives into unrighteousness.

Discipline in Christ prepares us for eternal life
and regret born resentment of life.

Become a tree and have a trunk of discipline.

Let regret be like grass that withers in the winter.

Discipline me, Lord, and save me forever.

Paint Your Future
with
Practical Points for Reflection

List three words that best describe what this poem means to your life.

1. _____.

2. _____.

3. _____.

After reading this poem, list three characteristics you want to change for the better.

1. _____.

2. _____.

3. _____.

Take-Action
Do things that will shape your future.

1. Do not put off today for tomorrow.
2. Listen to wise men and women.
3. Make your life goals a priority.
4. Set a date to complete a task.
5. Have a mind to grow and stop settling for less.
6. Start small, then increase.

Hebrews 12:11
Now no chastening for the present seemeth to be joyous,
but grievous: nevertheless, afterward, it yieldeth the peaceable
fruit of righteousness unto them which are exercised thereby.

Jesus, He's Available

Jesus is available when we are lost,

when we are lonely and scared,

when we become weary,

when we are sick or tired,

when your children go astray,

when we feel defeated and depressed,

when we are afraid and doubting.

Jesus is available to put us on the path of righteousness,

to give us happiness in our life,

to help us overcome sin,

to give us joy and peace,

to help us tell our families about the saving grace of Jesus.

Jesus is available to give us an everlasting praise and song.

Jesus is available

to make every crooked way in our life straight.

People of God let us all come available,

so Jesus can be available in our lives.

Paint Your Future
with
Practical Points for Reflection

List three words that best describe what this poem means to your life.

1. _____.

2. _____.

3. _____.

After reading this poem, list three characteristics you want to change for the better.

1. _____.

2. _____.

3. _____.

Take-Action
Do things that will shape your future.

1. Do not put off today for tomorrow.
2. Listen to wise men and women.
3. Make your life goals a priority.
4. Set a date to complete a task.
5. Have a mind to grow and stop settling for less.
6. Start small, then increase.

Isaiah 6:8
"Also, I heard the voice of the Lord, saying, Whom shall I send,
and who will go for us? Then said I, Here *am* I; send me."

Never Alone

We are never alone when we reach out to God and his people.

When you are driving down a dusty road or when you

are lost and weary.

We are never alone when it is time to make a tough

decision or when your faith is low.

We are never alone when we are at school, work, or church.

We are never alone during praise and worship.

We are never alone during times of sickness and death.

We are never alone because

God is always with us through his Holy Spirit.

Never alone is not ever being alone with Jesus.

Paint Your Future
with
Practical Points for Reflection

List three words that best describe what this poem means to your life.

1. _____.

2. _____.

3. _____.

After reading this poem, list three characteristics you want to change for the better.

1. _____.

2. _____.

3. _____.

Take-Action

Do things that will shape your future.

1. Do not put off today for tomorrow.
2. Listen to wise men and women.
3. Make your life goals a priority.
4. Set a date to complete a task.
5. Have a mind to grow and stop settling for less.
6. Start small, then increase.

Isaiah 41:10
"Fear thou not; for I *am* with thee: be not dismayed; for I *am* thy God:
I will strengthen thee; yea, I will help thee; yea,
I will uphold thee with the right hand of my righteousness."

No Longer Buried in Sin

Children of God show the world how good it feels to be

delivered from sin.

God will cloth you with love, joy, and peace and take,

away your sins.

What a blessing it is to enter the house of God ready to worship the Lord

because you are no longer buried in sin.

The power of the Holy Spirit, preaching and teaching of

the Gospel,

and faith in God's word will help you to escape sin.

We must humble ourselves to the word of God,

and

forsake everything not to be buried in sin.

Paint Your Future
with
Practical Points for Reflection

List three words that best describe what this poem means to your life.

1. _____.

2. _____.

3. _____.

After reading this poem, list three characteristics you want to change for the better.

1. _____.

2. _____.

3. _____.

Take-Action
Do things that will shape your future.

1. Do not put off today for tomorrow.
2. Listen to wise men and women.
3. Make your life goals a priority.
4. Set a date to complete a task.
5. Have a mind to grow and stop settling for less.
6. Start small, then increase.

James 5:16
Confess your faults one to another, and pray one for another,
that ye may be healed. The effectual fervent prayer of a righteous man availeth much.

Take it Back

Take back control of your household. Take it back from the devil.

Take back the parenthood of your children.

Take it Back!

Take back the love you had for your husband, wife, and family.

Take it Back!

Take back your place in society.

Take back your salvation in Jesus Christ.

Take it Back!

Take back the love you had for the church,
your neighborhood, society, and country. Take it Back!

Take back your health.

Take back your dreams and hope in Jesus,

Take it Back!

Take back your humble spirit.

Take back your mind, smile, and good looks.

Take back your money.

Saints of God, whatever the devil took from you, go back and get it.

Take it Back!

Paint Your Future
with
Practical Points for Reflection

List three words that best describe what this poem means to your life.

1. _____.

2. _____.

3. _____.

After reading this poem, list three characteristics you want to change for the better.

1. _____.

2. _____.

3. _____.

Take-Action
Do things that will shape your future.

1. Do not put off today for tomorrow.
2. Listen to wise men and women.
3. Make your life goals a priority.
4. Set a date to complete a task.
5. Have a mind to grow and stop settling for less.
6. Start small, then increase.

John 10:10
"The thief cometh not, but for to steal, and to kill,
and to destroy: I have come that they might have life,
and that they might have *it* more abundantly."

The Devil Thought He Had a Trap Set

The devil always thinks he can set a trap for God's people.

The trap may be set, but God protects his people from all danger.

The devil's trap is set for destruction, but the hands of God will
pull his people through it.

The devil's trap wants to condemn God's children for eternity.

The devil's trap is to keep us in the bondage of debt,
but God says debt-free.

The devil traps want the children of God to depend on him,
and deny God's power through his son Jesus,

The devil do not want the church to hear the word of God.

The devil trap do not want believers to give their tithes and offering.
to stop having faith in Jesus,
and to stop them from living a righteous life,

The devil wants to destroy everyone who is born of God
and stop anyone who wants to become his child.

The only trap the devil set was his own.

Paint Your Future
with
Practical Points for Reflection

List three words that best describe what this poem means to your life.

1. _____.

2. _____.

3. _____.

After reading this poem, list three characteristics you want to change for the better.

1. _____.

2. _____.

3. _____.

Take-Action
Do things that will shape your future.

1. Do not put off today for tomorrow.
2. Listen to wise men and women.
3. Make your life goals a priority.
4. Set a date to complete a task.
5. Have a mind to grow and stop settling for less.
6. Start small, then increase.

Galatians 5:1
"Stand fast therefore in the liberty wherewith Christ hath made us free,
and be not entangled again with the yoke of bondage."

It Happened at The Cross

God's endless love, mercy, and grace happened at the cross.

Jesus's public execution happened at the cross.

Jesus's blood redeems humanity back
to God happened at the cross.

Jesus's defeated sin, Satan, and the grave at the cross.

Jesus's death allowed us to escape God's wrath
of eternal damnation happened at the cross.

Jesus's blood delivered us from
evil happened at the cross.

Jesus gave us God's grace so that we

can have an abundant life now and eternal
life forever happened at the cross.

Jesus gave us victory over sin that happened at the cross.

Jesus gave us salvation that happened at the cross.

Jesus's blood on the cross paid the penalty for our sins
once and for all times happened at the cross.

Paint Your Future
with
Practical Points for Reflection

List three words that best describe what this poem means to your life.

1. _____.

2. _____.

3. _____.

After reading this poem, list three characteristics you want to change for the better.

1. _____.

2. _____.

3. _____.

Take-Action
Do things that will shape your future.

1. Do not put off today for tomorrow.
2. Listen to wise men and women.
3. Make your life goals a priority.
4. Set a date to complete a task.
5. Have a mind to grow and stop settling for less.
6. Start small, then increase.

2 Corinthians 5:21
"For he hath made him to be sin for us, who knew no sin;
that we might be made the righteousness of God in him."

Here's Your Prescription

We have been misused and abused by the people
in this world, but Jesus gave us his prescription.

Divine medicine of endless love, joy, peace, patience,
kindness, faithfulness, gentleness, and self-control.

When you are frustrated about something,
ask Jesus to give you a prescription for rest.

When people are trying to steal your self-esteem,

ask Jesus to give you a prescription for confidence.

Your friends are leading you into temptation
that is not wholesome, ask Jesus to give you
a prescription for peacemaking.

You are depressed at school because
no one wants to be your friend.

Ask Jesus to give you a prescription
to befriend like-minded people.

When your faith is tossed like a tropical storm wind;
here is your prescription for contentment.

Your life is on and off like the backyard water hose.
Here is your prescription of steadfastness.

You neglect your discipleship over the things of this world;
Here is your prescription for obedience.

Accept your spiritual transformation to come out
of the darkness and see the light of God.

God is the only one who has your prescription for divine change.

Paint Your Future
with
Practical Points for Reflection

List three words that best describe what this poem means to your life.

1. _____.

2. _____.

3. _____.

After reading this poem, list three characteristics you want to change for the better.

1. _____.

2. _____.

3. _____.

Take-Action
Do things that will shape your future.

1. Do not put off today for tomorrow.
2. Listen to wise men and women.
3. Make your life goals a priority.
4. Set a date to complete a task.
5. Have a mind to grow and stop settling for less.
6. Start small, then increase.

Psalms 119:103
"How sweet are thy words unto my taste! *yea, sweeter* than honey to my mouth!"

Be Ready

Be ready to worship God in trust and spirit.

Ready to tell the world the reasons why
you believe in Jesus's birth, life,

death, and resurrection.

Ready to confess your faith to those who are lost.

Ready to tell people their souls are at stake.

Ready to tell everyone how you found your purpose in life.

Ready to give your testimony on how you meet Jesus.

Ready To tell them how your sins no longer control your life.

Ready to tell them how you were baptized with the Holy Spirit.

Ready to fight a good fight until fight.

Ready to sing that last song to God.

Ready to pray in all situations.

Ready to witness to those who are lost.

Ready to accept your divine assignment,

for God's kingdom.

Are you ready for your eternal life with God?

Get Ready, Be Ready!

Paint Your Future
with
Practical Points for Reflection

List three words that best describe what this poem means to your life.

1. _____.

2. _____.

3. _____.

After reading this poem, list three characteristics you want to change for the better.

1. _____.

2. _____.

3. _____.

Take-Action

Do things that will shape your future.

1. Do not put off today for tomorrow.
2. Listen to wise men and women.
3. Make your life goals a priority.
4. Set a date to complete a task.
5. Have a mind to grow and stop settling for less.
6. Start small, then increase.

Matthew 24:44
"Therefore be ye also ready: for in such an hour as ye think not the Son of man cometh."

How Bad do You Want it?

Do you want it bad enough to fast for it?

To change for it?

To heal from sin?

To deliver you from drugs or alcohol?

To give you spiritual sight?

To hear the eternal words of God?

To live a righteous life?

To speak words of life and not death?

To end your suffering of physical pain?

To seek spiritual gifts to help win souls and change lives for

the sake of the kingdom?

To be spiritually transformed?

To suffer for it?

To serve others and God?

To be disciplined for it and obey God's commandment?

To worship with other believers and become a disciple?

Will you cry out for it?

Sacrifice for it? or will you believe all things are possible,

through Jesus?

How Bad do You Want It?

Paint Your Future
with
Practical Points for Reflection

List three words that best describe what this poem means to your life.

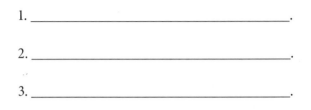

1. _____.

2. _____.

3. _____.

After reading this poem, list three characteristics you want to change for the better.

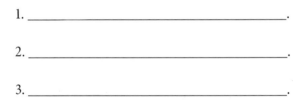

1. _____.

2. _____.

3. _____.

Take-Action
Do things that will shape your future.

1. Do not put off today for tomorrow.
2. Listen to wise men and women.
3. Make your life goals a priority.
4. Set a date to complete a task.
5. Have a mind to grow and stop settling for less.
6. Start small, then increase.

Acts 4:12
Neither is their salvation in any other:
for there is none other name under heaven given among men,
whereby we must be saved.

Another Day

It is a day we celebrate the life, death, burial, and
resurrection of of our Lord and Savior.

It is a day we encourage each other to stay in the faith.

A day we repent from our sins and ask forgiveness.

A day not to be reckless and careless with our lives.

A day to operate in the Fruit of the Spirit
and bring joy to someone's life.

A day to help those who are lost, hungry, and sick.

A day we get a chance to sing a song of victory
when life struggle comes, with tragedy.

It is a day we all allow Jesus to change our hearts
from the ways of this world to the ways of God.

It is a day we will worship God in his eternal presence.

It is a day we will forgive those who hurt use verbally and physically.

It is not just another day, but a day to be like Jesus.

Paint Your Future
with
Practical Points for Reflection

List three words that best describe what this poem means to your life.

1. _____.

2. _____.

3. _____.

After reading this poem, list three characteristics you want to change for the better.

1. _____.

2. _____.

3. _____.

Take-Action
Do things that will shape your future.

1. Do not put off today for tomorrow.
2. Listen to wise men and women.
3. Make your life goals a priority.
4. Set a date to complete a task.
5. Have a mind to grow and stop settling for less.
6. Start small, then increase.

Psalms 118:24
"This is the day which the LORD hath made;
we will rejoice and be glad in it."

Win

Winners are not people who finish first but those who complete the race.

Winner work at obtaining the imperishable crown of eternal life.

Winners do what it takes to accomplish their goals.

Winners are those who try a task before labeling themselves as a loser.

Winners do not give up easily, but they come up with ways to be successful.

Winners get involved in things that are bigger than themselves.

Winners share joy and happiness with someone besides themselves.

Winners make themselves available for those who are lost.

Winners do not hold animosity, but they
share their talents to spawn champions.

Winners propel families, teams, groups,
and individuals towards victory.

Winners focus on righteousness.

Winners sometimes must lose to appreciate,

the life God has given to them.

A winner personality is like a locomotive train
whispering at every turn to be noticed.

Winners lead with a servant attitude.

Winners grow old to be a blessing to others.

A winner is not a brand name but a character name

that receives the prize of eternal life.

Do you want to win?

Paint Your Future
with
Practical Points for Reflection

List three words that best describe what this poem means to your life.

1. _____.

2. _____.

3. _____.

After reading this poem, list three characteristics you want to change for the better.

1. _____.

2. _____.

3. _____.

Take-Action
Do things that will shape your future.

1. Do not put off today for tomorrow.
2. Listen to wise men and women.
3. Make your life goals a priority.
4. Set a date to complete a task.
5. Have a mind to grow and stop settling for less.
6. Start small, then increase.

Luke 18:27
And he said, The things which are impossible with men are possible with God.

Scare to Move

Why are we still in the same position since last year?

Because we are not able to move from

carnality to spirituality,

from mortal life to living life on purpose,

from your life plan to Jesus's plan for your life.

Because we are scared to move.

Why are we accepting defeat instead of victory?

accepting a fruitless life instead of a product life,

accepting a self-will life instead of Jesus's plan for your life.

Because we are scared to move.

Why are we not turning from mortality to immortality?

from a life of corruption to incorruption?

from a lover of self to loving Jesus,

from a hostage life to a life of praise?

Because we are scared to move.

Why are we highlighting our titles, degrees, and pride in life?

We love the sinner's life instead of a saved life.

To be with Jesus, you must move in his direction.

God is moving, Jesus is moving, and the Holy Spirit is moving.

Now, when are you going to move?

Paint Your Future
with
Practical Points for Reflection

List three words that best describe what this poem means to your life.

1. _____.

2. _____.

3. _____.

After reading this poem, list three characteristics you want to change for the better.

1. _____.

2. _____.

3. _____.

Take-Action
Do things that will shape your future.

1. Do not put off today for tomorrow.
2. Listen to wise men and women.
3. Make your life goals a priority.
4. Set a date to complete a task.
5. Have a mind to grow and stop settling for less.
6. Start small, then increase.

2 Timothy 1:7
"For God hath not given us the spirit of fear, but of power,
and of love, and of a sound mind."

POEMS OF LAMENT

Missing You Jesus

Missing Jesus is like missing momma's pound cake
with butter, cream frosting,

or the birth of your first grandchild,

or loss of a body part in a war fight.

Missing Jesus is like being absent from church,

or your Holy Ghost fire.

Missing Jesus is like life has lost its hoorah moments,

or the taste of peace, love, and joy in the Holy Spirit.

Missing Jesus is like missing the gates to get into Heaven,

or receiving the gift of salvation.

Missing you, Jesus is like missing your grace

that is greater than any love,

a woman or man can give.

All these things remind me what it is like,

when we are missing you, Jesus.

Paint Your Future
with
Practical Points for Reflection

List three words that best describe what this poem means to your life.

1. _____.

2. _____.

3. _____.

After reading this poem, list three characteristics you want to change for the better.

1. _____.

2. _____.

3. _____.

Take-Action
Do things that will shape your future.

1. Do not put off today for tomorrow.
2. Listen to wise men and women.
3. Make your life goals a priority.
4. Set a date to complete a task.
5. Have a mind to grow and stop settling for less.
6. Start small, then increase.

Psalms 16:11
"Thou wilt shew me the path of life: in thy presence is fulness of joy;
at thy right hand, there are pleasures forevermore."

No Peace

What do you do when there is no peace?

Where do you go when there is no peace?

Whom do you see when there is no peace?

How do you handle your situation

when there is no peace?

You have done everything to have harmony in your life,

yet, you have no peace.

You have pain in your body because there is no peace.

You have developed a disease because there is no peace.

Children perform poorly at school,

because there is no peace at home.

Families cannot share their love for one another,

because there is no peace.

No peace brings about resentment and regret.

No peace becomes a scare in your mind,

and a bullet in your heart.

You no longer lament over the problems,

in your life because you

accepted the peace of Jesus,

and no man can take it away.

Paint Your Future
with
Practical Points for Reflection

List three words that best describe what this poem means to your life.

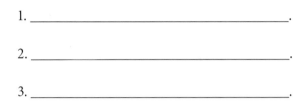

1. _____.

2. _____.

3. _____.

After reading this poem, list three characteristics you want to change for the better.

1. _____.

2. _____.

3. _____.

Take-Action
Do things that will shape your future.

1. Do not put off today for tomorrow.
2. Listen to wise men and women.
3. Make your life goals a priority.
4. Set a date to complete a task.
5. Have a mind to grow and stop settling for less.
6. Start small, then increase.

John 14:27
"Peace I leave with you, my peace I give unto you: not as the world giveth,
give I unto you. Let not your heart be troubled, neither let it be afraid."

Silence

Silence is good when you want to hear a word from God.

Silence is the unbiblical cord to God's precepts.

Silence does not always come from the giver but the receiver.

Silence can catch you off guard when you want to talk.

Silence is not an act of love but a way
to distance yourself from the ungodly.

Silence will teach you how to watch and pray.

Silence will allow you to hear God when the world is at war.

Silence will help you hear and see the good in someone.

Silence will allow you to search your soul for the things of God.

Silence is not dead but very much alive.

Do not be silent to the sins of this world but blow the

trumpet of salvation and let everybody know
Jesus saves you, from your sins.

Paint Your Future
with
Practical Points for Reflection

List three words that best describe what this poem means to your life.

1. _____.

2. _____.

3. _____.

After reading this poem, list three characteristics you want to change for the better.

1. _____.

2. _____.

3. _____.

Take-Action
Do things that will shape your future.

1. Do not put off today for tomorrow.
2. Listen to wise men and women.
3. Make your life goals a priority.
4. Set a date to complete a task.
5. Have a mind to grow and stop settling for less.
6. Start small, then increase.

Ecclesiastes 9:17
"The words of wise men are heard in quiet more than
the cry of him that ruleth among fools."

Unveil

Let us unveil the truth about Satan
by living the ways, of God.

Unveil the things in your life that is not of God.

Unveil the deeds of the devil and

annihilate them with God's words.

Unveil ungodly people, places,

and things that are blocking your

blessings.

Unveil everything that does not represent the truth of God.

Unveil emotions and feeling that trouble your soul.

Unveil the enemy as he set up roadblocks,

to block your path of righteousness.

Unveil the devil by asking Jesus to destroy

the things he had planned for your life.

Ask God to unveil your stubborn mind,

of excepting a little when,

God's have abundance for your life.

Unveil the mask of the devil and

expose his evil deeds to the world.

Paint Your Future
with
Practical Points for Reflection

List three words that best describe what this poem means to your life.

1. _____.

2. _____.

3. _____.

After reading this poem, list three characteristics you want to change for the better.

1. _____.

2. _____.

3. _____.

Take-Action
Do things that will shape your future.

1. Do not put off today for tomorrow.
2. Listen to wise men and women.
3. Make your life goals a priority.
4. Set a date to complete a task.
5. Have a mind to grow and stop settling for less.
6. Start small, then increase.

1 Corinthians 10:21
"Ye cannot drink the cup of the Lord, and the cup of devils:
ye cannot be partakers of the Lord's table, and of the table of devils."

Tarnish

We are tarnish because we are not steadfast in God's words.

We are not delighting in his statutes.

We do not give God fervent prays.

Is this you?

We guide ourselves.

We are disobedient to God's commandments.

We lack in servicing with our time, talents, and treasures.

Is this you?

We forget to love one another.

We focus on ourselves and not Jesus.

We are chasing after the things of this world.

Is this you?

We abuse our lifestyle of holiness and replace it with idolatry.

We experience fear of losing our worldly friends.

We fellowship more with the world than your church family.

Is this you?

We are torn between two worlds. One of right now pleasure

and the other is yet to come.

It will come a day to decide to serve God with all our heart, mind, and soul.

Instead of being tarnished, we will be as bright
as the star that everyone, wants to follow. Is this you?

Paint Your Future
with
Practical Points for Reflection

List three words that best describe what this poem means to your life.

1. _____.

2. _____.

3. _____.

After reading this poem, list three characteristics you want to change for the better.

1. _____.

2. _____.

3. _____.

Take-Action
Do things that will shape your future.

1. Do not put off today for tomorrow.
2. Listen to wise men and women.
3. Make your life goals a priority.
4. Set a date to complete a task.
5. Have a mind to grow and stop settling for less.
6. Start small, then increase.

Galatians 6:8
For he that soweth to his flesh shall of the flesh reap corruption.
but he that soweth to the Spirit shall of the Spirit reap life everlasting.

Knock Down, But Not Out

Alarming information has a way of catching you off guard.

You listen to the local news that reports more bad news than good.

You find out the woman who raised you is not your mother.

Knocked down but not knocked out.

You find out your coworker got the promotion over you.

Your grandfather died in a car accident on your birthday.

You practiced for four months to be on the
basketball varsity team, but you were cut.

Knockdown but not knock out.

You are unhappy for reasons A through Z.

You are discouraged because things did not go your way.

Knocked down but not knocked out.

You are closer to Jesus, but your enemy wants to kill you.

You sometimes listen to the cares of this world
and forget about Jesus, supplying your needs.

You forget to invite others to church to have dinner with Jesus.

Knocked down but not knocked out.

Your sister got cancer, so you start to doubt your faith.

You are grieving over the loss of your math teacher.

You are agonizing now over the loss of your job.

Knocked down but not knocked out.

You will sing songs of victory to comfort you
in times of trouble confusion, and depression.

With Jesus on your side, you will never be knocked out!

Paint Your Future
with
Practical Points for Reflection

List three words that best describe what this poem means to your life.

1. _____.

2. _____.

3. _____.

After reading this poem, list three characteristics you want to change for the better.

1. _____.

2. _____.

3. _____.

Take-Action
Do things that will shape your future.

1. Do not put off today for tomorrow.
2. Listen to wise men and women.
3. Make your life goals a priority.
4. Set a date to complete a task.
5. Have a mind to grow and stop settling for less.
6. Start small, then increase.

1 Corinthians 9:25
And every man that striveth for mastery is temperate in all things.
Now they do it to obtain a corruptible crown; but we incorruptible.

Burn

You were serving God well, but your fire went out.

It was smoldered by someone tall and handsome,

or she was beautiful and smelled like perfume.

It was torched by the negative comments coming from a selected few.

You have been burned.

You are scorched by giving your time to following ungodly things.

You were mar by unforgiveness of past hurts and pains.

You speak death instead of life into your life.

You have been burned.

You were inflamed by the things of this world
and the immediate comfort from it.

You became blazed with anxiety attacks when asked to do kingdom work.

You are in a crossfire between loving God and the world.

You have been burned.

It was a firestorm of life circumstances that drew you back to the world.

You lost your job to a bush fire.

It was a wildfire of suffering losses that drew you away from God.

You have been burned.

When your obedience to Christ become like a fiery furnace

no scheme can burn you or stop God's blessing for your life.

Paint Your Future
with
Practical Points for Reflection

List three words that best describe what this poem means to your life.

1. _____.

2. _____.

3. _____.

After reading this poem, list three characteristics you want to change for the better.

1. _____.

2. _____.

3. _____.

Take-Action

Do things that will shape your future.

1. Do not put off today for tomorrow.
2. Listen to wise men and women.
3. Make your life goals a priority.
4. Set a date to complete a task.
5. Have a mind to grow and stop settling for less.
6. Start small, then increase.

Isaiah 53:5
But he was wounded for our transgressions, he was bruised for our iniquities:
the chastisement of our peace was upon him; and with his stripes we are healed.

Raise Your Hands

Things in life are not going right, but Jesus says, raise your hands.

Raise your hands for Jesus to take you out of your troubles.

Raise your hands if you are lost and scared?

Raise your hands and voice so Jesus can find you.

Raise your hands and surrender to the will, protection, and the

provision Jesus has for your life.

You throw a brick into someone else life,

but you told Jesus it was you who did it.

Jesus said, raise your hands and ask forgiveness.

Raise your hands to receive salvation,

the Holy Spirit, and faith in Jesus.

Jesus, I raise my hands to ask you to please help me.

Every time there is sadness, discomfort,

and persecution in my life,

I know I can raise my hands and live for that day.

I will raise my hands against iniquity,
jealousy, hatred, violence, and strife.

I will raise my hands to serve God and his people.

I will raise my hands to receive God's healing

I decided to raise my hands to Jesus and live.

Paint Your Future
with
Practical Points for Reflection

List three words that best describe what this poem means to your life.

1. _____.

2. _____.

3. _____.

After reading this poem, list three characteristics you want to change for the better.

1. _____.

2. _____.

3. _____.

Take-Action
Do things that will shape your future.

1. Do not put off today for tomorrow.
2. Listen to wise men and women.
3. Make your life goals a priority.
4. Set a date to complete a task.
5. Have a mind to grow and stop settling for less.
6. Start small, then increase.

Psalm 28:2
Hear the voice of my supplications when I cry to unto thee,
when I lift my hands toward thy holy oracle.

Printed in the United States
by Baker & Taylor Publisher Services